David Austin, Luther Pratt

The Dance of Herodias, through the Streets of Hartford, on Election Day

To the Tune of the Stars of Heaven, in the Dragon's Tail

David Austin, Luther Pratt

The Dance of Herodias, through the Streets of Hartford, on Election Day
To the Tune of the Stars of Heaven, in the Dragon's Tail

ISBN/EAN: 9783337149208

Printed in Europe, USA, Canada, Australia, Japan

Cover: Foto ©ninafisch / pixelio.de

More available books at **www.hansebooks.com**

DANCE OF HERODIAS,

Through the Streets of Hartford,

ON

ELECTION DAY,

TO THE TUNE OF

THE STARS OF HEAVEN, IN THE

DRAGON's TAIL;

O R,

A gentle trip at the heels of the Strumpet of Babylon.

Playing tricks in the attire of the

Daughters of Zion.

PRINTED FOR THE AUTHOR.

1799.

CHURCH AND STATE CONNECTED.

" THE church and state together blended,
      Make an appearance very splendid.
Like *mystery Babyl'n the great*
Magnificently cloth'd in state.
Or like th' apocalyptic Harlot
When deck'd with gold and dress'd in scarlet.
At Hartford, may be seen, at Election
The likeness shewn to great perfection,
When her procession will appear
with all the clergy in the rear*;
Who, while the music plays, will lag on,
As drags along his tail, the Dragon.
While num'rous Guards in armour bright,
Well disciplin'd, and taught to fight,
Attend the process, on the road,
From Court-House to the House of God:
Where Priests and Statesmen take their places
And put on sanctimonious faces.
And lend, awhile, a candid ear
To solemn councils which they hear.
(But what most forcibly impresses,
Are plaudits in the last addresses.)
    The service clos'd, after amen,
The Guards escort her back again.
Thus ends the curious exibition
Of what is destin'd to perdition.

This hetrogenious compoſition,
And grand ſupport of impoſition,
Emphatically ſtyl'd THE WHORE,
Will ſoon expire, and be no more.
This *Auſtin* finds in Revelation,
And boldly makes the proclamation :
But leſt the truth ſhould credit gain,
The Clergy cry—" *The man's inſane.*"

SIR,

The foregoing ludicrous poem, compoſed merely for the author's own amuſement, is now tranſmitted to you, by deſire of ſeveral of your unknown friends, as a token of their reſpect, and the entire approbation they feel of the ſentiments they have heard you deliver, and with the warmeſt wiſhes that you may be ſucceeded, and be happily inſtrumental in diffuſing light, and liberating the world from thoſe ſhackles of ſuperſtition and bigotry, by which they have been bound down in ſervile ſubmiſſion to antichriſtian power, and impell'd to *worſhip* THE BEAST, *or his image.*

Thoſe who are intoxicated with the cup of the whore of Babylon, will no doubt, take every method in their power to prejudice the minds of the people againſt you, and if poſſible, deſtroy your influence.—But in ſpite of all their efforts,

truth will finally prevail—*Babylon must fall!*
The whore already begins to be hated; and will
soon be made *desolate and naked—and her flesh*
will be eaten.—she shall be burnt with fire, and
utterly confumed. *For strong is the LORD GOD*
who judgeth her.

Mr. Auſtin.   May 1798.

Copy of a Memorial, to be prefented to the
General Affembly of the ſtate of Connecti-
cut, at their October Seſſions: to be held at
New-Haven—A. D. 1799.

Gentlemen of the Houſe of Repreſentatives,

SIRS,

AT a period when the kingdoms of the earth
are tottering, and the nations *are angry*
becauſe the time of the judgments of GOD are
come; it will ſcarcely be thought trefpaffing on
your time, or infulting to your wiſdom, if a mo-
ments attention be requeſted to the intereſting
ſubject, concerning which the nations are now
agitating; on account of which the thunders of
Heaven are now rolling; and before which tem-
peſt, *myſtical Babylon* is falling.

An inveſtigation of the ground of controverſy,
now ſo cloſely preſſed, between the GOD of
providence, and the kingdoms of this world
cannot be deemed an object unworthy of the

ablest pen, or the most eloquent tongue. The
ground of controversy as it respects the realms
of the *papal* throne hath been ably controvert-
ed. It is not denied but the *cup* of the *mystical
whore* is formed by her fellowship with the
" kings of the earth." That this fellowship
exists in the texture of the " *politico, ecclesiasti-
ac*, establishments" of the papal see, the scriptures declare; and the same sentiment was ever
breathed forth in the lectures of the late presi-
dent Stiles on the subject of ecclesiastical history,
in unison with this exposition of the prophetic
writings all protestant writers of note, both in
Europe and America have pronounced their
decisions. Of consequence there is, with the
intelligent, no difficulty in uniting with the an-
thems of inspiration, *saying*, (imputable to the
downfall of the nations within the limits of the
papal power) *we give thee thanks O LORD GOD
Almighty, which art and wast and art to come, because thou hast taken to thee thy great power and
hast reigned, and the nations were angry, and thy
wrath is come, and the time of the dead that they
should be judged.* All this, protestants allow to
be good and wholesome doctrine in reference to
the first branch of the antichristian household—
to " the MOTHER OF HARLOTS"—to the " woman that sitteth upon many waters"—" with
whom the kings of the earth have committed

fornication"—"that sitteth upon a *scarlet colored*
(a persecuting) BEAST, full of names of blas-
phemy" (of reproaches against the simplicity of
the gospel worship and order) " having seven
heads and ten horns"—a figure of *civil and ecclesiastical* power in papal Rome.

AGAINST such a power as this, protestant di-
vines have no objection to the going forth of the
thunders of Heaven, in full detail. But now
comes the controversial pill. A recent and just
interpretation of the prophetic characters de-
clares, that the same guilt which is laid at the
door of the *papal* household, arising from her
connection with the " kings of the earth,"
must be disposed of by those who imitate her example in the *protestant* department. At this
charge our Clergy take umbrage and say ; will
you, then, dislodge us from the arms, embraces,
and supports of civil power ? calling these sui-
tors, "kings of the earth," *rivals* of the King
of Kings, and intruders into the bed-chamber of
the Heavenly Bridegroom ? and of consequence
infer, that we are lying in the bosom of Herod."
Let the fact answer for itself ! for tho' this pros-
titute woman have a daughter whose name is
" Herodias," whose movements are graceful and
exceedingly entertaining to by-standers on Herod's birth day—while she dress her train and

parade them in military order on election days, and tho' she preach moft eloquent fermons, fuch as delight the ear of Herod, and finally, in a fet of complimentary phrafes, advance him and his train to Heaven like the papal bifhop at the fall of Lewis the fixteenth, who, to confole the fufferer under his unexpected fate, from the charriot of papal elevation cried out " Louis feize fil de Louis quatorze, montez au ciel ! —Louis feize fil de Louis quatorze, montez auciel !*—yet it may be, this graceful dame may be a daughter of Babylon after all. Let Herod afk of her her reward for this fervice, and being inftructed of her mo.. ther, it is a hazzard, but fhe will ftill fay—*give me here the head of John the Babtift in a charger !*—Cut off the head, or bear down all teftimony againft the connexion between the mother and the royal favor !"

SIRS,

In the light of this uncontrovertable prophetic afpect, your memorialift prefents for your confideration the following queftions :

1. Do not the eftablifhments of religion which now exifts, either in the form or under the pat-

---

* *Lewis the fixteenth, fon of Lewis the fourteenth, afcend up to Heaven !*

ronage of monarchical or national favor, look much like sproutings from the papal stump?

2. If the indignation of Heaven is pouring forth for the purification of the mystical whore, doth it not well become the protestant daughters forthwith to purify their garments?

3. If the politico, ecclesiastico stars of the *papal* firmament, for their unasked aid, like Uzzah, have been struck from there heights, will it not become all protestant interference to withdraw its hand, before the indignation of incensed Heaven break forth?

4. Might not all the laws* of the state of Connecticut respecting ecclesiastical concerns be repealed, without contravening the spirit of the truth, or the present order of providence, or endangering the safety of the ark of GOD?

A *descendant* of DAVID.

---

* THE laws referred to are all acts, or paragraphs in acts, by which the visible ministers of the gospel are made ministers of the state :— by which the support of the gospel presumed to belong to the state, and which levy taxes by state authority for that purpose : by which the existence, of the Kingdom of the Redeemer is solemnly represented as incapable to support itself : or christians, slanderously, represented as indisposed of their own free will, to contribute, ...

To the members of the General Assembly &c.

SIRS,

WILL it be thought matter of presumption, or of indelicacy that a glance of the eye should be requested to the following hints in aid to the memorial, on the subject of the repeal of all the laws of the state of Connecticut, which either directly, or indirectly, innocently or wickedly, form that encircling embrace which hath doomed to prostitution the christian bride, now laboring to recover the native rights of an Heavenborn maid?

By a repeal of these laws, you will

1. EXONORATE yourselves from the charge of a presumptuous interference in the concerns of the kingdom of GOD; and, possibly, save

cording as GOD may have p_____ *them*, to the support of that g___l in which their hope rests.

These laws and sections of laws are such as affirm, as belonging to the state, the whole prerogative of ecclesiastical adjudication: such as make it the duty of ecclesiastical societies " to apply to the County Court in the County where such society is situate, to appoint and fix the place whereon their meeting-house shall be erected and built "—as oblige the clerk of the society on the penalty of " seven dollars to certify the county court of the doings of said society," as authorize the assembly, in case " of complaint from the county court, to assess such tax on the yourſelves from the ſtroke which brought Uriah to the ground —which drave Uriah from the altar, and chaſed him before the avenging earthquake, as the papal intruders have been chaſed before the earthquake, of the French Revolution : hapleſs *rivals* of Jehovah's ſon !

2. You would afford opportunity for evidence to declare that your attention to this celeſtial

---

ſociety as they ſhall judge proper for the carrying on and finiſhing the meeting-houſe thus begun :" as forbid. religious ſocieties from entering upon the building of an houſe for the worſhip of God, without firſt obtaining permiſſion of, and falling under the eye, of the preſcribing county court, " under the penalty of one hundred and thirty four dollars for every tranſgreſſion. And ſuch county court ſhall be allowed the fees for their judgment thereon, as in the trial of other cauſ- es." *Stat. Con.* p. 294. 5.

This memorial would demand the repeal of ſuch laws and ſections of laws, as forbid a perſon to act in the viſible concerns of his ſalvation, unleſs he have a certain legal qualification in point of *freehold eſtate—or rate in the liſt,* or he be a perſon in *full communion with the church in ſaid town,* as make it the duty of the *ſelect men of the town,* to ſee to it, that all taxes levied on this eccleſiaſtical houſe be *duly collected,* by demanding a writ *from juſtice of the peace or eſſelſment, for that purpoſe* ; as appoint aſſeſſors upon collectors not already in their duty in this concern ; as make the eſtates of the *ſelect men liable to diſtreſs* ; if they don't take out a diſtreſs upon the collectors or collectors as aforeſaid, together with a line of the maid was founded on purer principles than thofe of ftate policy, or of perfonal accommodation. The enemy, no longer, fhould fay that the miniftry founded your praife, in return for the Babylonifh garment and the wedge of gold you aided them to hide in the bottom of the tent.

3. You would wreft from the hand of the enemy a moft deadly lance, which, with too much fuccefs, he wields againft the purity and inno-cency of revealed truth ; whilft he conftantly afferts that the labors of eftablifhed priefthood amount but to the merchandife of Babylon.——

dollars to the county *treafurer for every fuch neglect.*

At which fhall be received by action brought by the ftates attorney, to the county court, in the fame county, ; and no appeal fhall be granted in fuch cafe.

LET all fuch acts be ftruck down as authorize *an affiftant, or juftice of the peace,* next refiding to any town neglecting to choofe a collector or collectors for itfelf, *to appoint and empower by his warrant, fuch collector* or *collectors for the town aforefaid.*——All fuch acts as fecure to a minifter, not wanted in his parifh, the right of applying to the affembly for the maintainance which the people choofe not to afford : and alfo, all fuch acts as lay fines, demand fums or pay-ments from congregations which, for caufes well known to themfelves, fhall not choofe to fettle a minifter, *according to law* within a giv-en time.   *Stat. Con. p.* 315. 16. 17. 18. 19.

that such stars shine in borrowed light ; that the elements of their political firmament need only to be difolved, and the meteors will fall, as when a fig-tree is shaken of an untimely wind.

4. Were the foregoing affertion to prove true and the predicted effects to follow, moft happy opportunity would prefent for the wifdom and power and grace of the mighty Redeemer to exert itfelf in purifying his bride, in gathering his own into his own arms, and in forming to himfelf that kingdom, wherein dwelleth righteoufnefs. For this opportunity, and for this event, the whole creation now travaileth in birth and is pained to be delivered.

5. By preffing this proftitute from your bofem, you would awaken in her, if ought of delicate fentiments, and purity of attire remain, a poignant fenfe of the injury done to the honor of her Heavenly hufband, whilft fhe hath provoked his jeloufy, by reclining on the bofom of the " kings of the earth."—Should her celeftial lover receive her again, of which fhe need not doubt, the joy of the renewed efpoufal will, a thoufand fold, compenfate for the momentary grief of being loofed from the arms of an unlawful embrace.

C

6. You would greatly aid the introduction of the SECOND REVOLUTION which is *inward* and *spiritual* and which is founded on principles of e-vangelical purity ; forbiding the contaminating touch of the beast, or of his image to be received in the hand or in the forehead. **Let then the** tea, with a *tax upon it*, go into **the harbor of** Boston !

But, Sirs, you may be willing to hear an an-fwer to the objections, which might be brought against a compliance, with the prayer of the me-morial. Let then **the objection, from the heights** of our nominal zion, or rather, **from the zion** that *dwelleth with the daughter of Babylon* be heard.

1. THE trumpet announes, in trembling accents, " if you fap our foundation, you will foon fee an end to the christian religion "—*Arj*. As an infidel argument, this objection is answered, by a declaration that in regard to its *origin*, or means of *support* the Gospel kingdom is not of this world ; of consequence the withdrawing of political interference from the support of this kingdom, no more endangers its safety, than the removal of a foundation, on which the ed-fice never stood.

FROM the lips of a christian, such an objection its but the offspring of unbelief, and amounts to slander against the cause he professes to maintain. With the same justice it might be said that the ark of GOD, tho' under the auspices of Heaven, could never find its way thro' the waters of the Mediteranean, were it not for the stores and runing rigging, borrowed of the fleets of the different powers it met in the way. Such men can be but fresh-water sailors, tho' mitres, doctorates, and diplomas adorn their brow !

Obj. 2. But have we not enjoyed great tranquility during the period in which our church and state have thus walked in kind embrace ?

Ans. So has Rome Papal, as far as the thunder of her bulls, and of her arms, could suppress the testimony of the truth ; and consign to the inquisitions, to purgatory and to Hell all who questioned the lawfulness of her connection with the " kings of the earth !" Rome protestant hath defended herself on the same principles, tho' to the matter defended was attached all the corruptions of the mystical cup, of which the bright example is given in the person and character of the reforming head, Henry the eighth. *The time of this ignorance GOD hath winked at, but now commands all men every where to repent.*

Obj. 3. Will not great perfonal inconvenience arife from the meafure contemplated ?

Anf. No true ftar can be fhaken : only meteors will fall : and in refpect to fuch, why fhould controverfy be maintained, feeing the decree of Heaven is gone forth to roll the ftone, cut out without hands, againft the feet of the image which were of *iron and of clay ?*—If the wind of Heaven, like an irrefiftable tornado is gone, and is going over the face of the earth, becaufe the iniquity of the Amorites is full ; why fhould we be backward to take up the ark of God, in due order, and march in and take poffeffion of the goodly land ? *To whom fwear he that they fhould not enter into his reft but to them that believed not ?*

Obj. 4. WILL not fuch diffolving of church and ftate connection mar all our profpects, in refpect to the fpeedy introduction of the millenial eftate ?

Anf. Far otherwife !—It is the only way in which preparation for that happy event can be made. It is the removing of the rubbifh under which the old foundation lies. This foundation we muft look for. On this foundation we muft build. In all things muft we build according to the pattern fhewed to us in the mount. This pattern is pure in doctrine, and in precept and in discipline. Let, then, the old fabric, by gentle agreement be taken down, lest *our river be dried up* that *the way of the kings of the east be prepared.* The same rod which hath broken the incrustation of other nations, may, in GOD's hand, demand of us the *liberation of the captives;* in case the milder methods of rational and of scriptural demand do not succeed.

IN the light of these collateral considerations, can there, sirs!—remain a shadow of doubt whether the voice of the truth, of GOD, and of your own safety do not demand a ready and cheerful compliance with the spirit of the memorial presented?

A descendant of DAVID.

P. S. THAT no unfair management may be ever complained of, in the prosecution of the spirit of this memorial, all doctors of divinity with all their *subordinate aid;* all associations, confociations, councils and councellors, whether already assembled or to be assembled, are hereby notified that the objects of this memorial will be prosecuted before the honorable General Assembly, as soon as the business of the session will admit of an easy introduction of the memorial, and their indulgence admit of a hearing in its support.

18

The DOUBTS, &c.

The doubts which might arise in the minds of any in respect to the propriety of the publication of the foregoing, with design to strike down the stars which shine in borrowed light; to whom hope seemed to be granted that they might still hold their place, will be dispelled; when it be considered that the jealousies of Heaven are aroused afresh; by a *palpable denial* of the truth and justice of the prophetic application, which brings "the stars" of our firmament into the family of " the mother of harlots :" by the contemptuous treatment which the notices of Heaven's gracious design were received: and by a fixed determination on the part of the priesthood to continue their present station, sentiments and course, rather than to roll their hopes and prospects upon the sustaining arm of the great head of the church.

The undersigned is commanded, again, to take the station he held whilst opening and applying the prophetic characters, to the visible clergy; of the state establishments which to them appertain; and to thunder against them the rebuke which their apostacy demands—that they, in the end, may know that God's holy word is as true and just in its sentence against them, as to other apostates of less-notoriety, and less capable to hide their iniquity under the skirts of the Babylonish garment.

To shew the justice of the sentence of God, in the prophecies, against the clergy of the political establishments; I dare to pronounce that in them, and in the spirit of their present ministry, the croakings of the *three unclean spirits* which came out of the mouth of the dragon, and out of the mouth of the beast, and out of the mouth of the false prophet, are found.

The evidence of this charge is discovered,

1. In a just construction of the prophetic figure,

2. In the course these spirits take, and in the object they have in view: and

3. In the impossibility of any other construction.

1. The just construction of the prophetic figure. *And I saw three unclean spirits like frogs come out of the mouth of the dragon, and out of the mouth of the beast, and out of the mouth of the false prophet.* By the dragon is to be understood *kingly power.* This is evident from the rank the dragon holds among beasts. He is king of all the beasts, or subordinate dragons of the field. Pharaoh is called the dragon, as lying in the fens beside the river of Egypt; and also, in the exclamation of the prophet. *Art not thou it that*

Ad cut Rahab and wounded the dragon ; that cut the land of Egypt by the many plagues, and wounded the *dragonic* power of Egypt in the perfon of Pharaoh and his hoft ? Satan is fometimes called the dragon, as the great dragon of dragons ; the great king of kings, the greet devil of devils in the apoftate fhades : on the dark fide of the queftion.

By the BEAST, underftand the dragonic power, bearing in its arms or carrying upon its fhoulders the apoftate woman, called the GREAT WHORE *which fitteth upon many waters, with whom the kings of the earth have committed forxication.* The apoftate church, in the arms of the ftate, forms the character of the BEAST. Thus when, in and after the reformation, the proteftant church reclined into the arms of the ftate ; fhe is chargeable, with her lovers, of taking the form of the IMAGE of the beaft.

FROM this dragonic and beaftly power combined, proceeds, as out of their mouth an adminiftration, that takes the character of the *falfe prophet.* This comprifes the teftimony of the whole combined priefthood in all fections of kingly chriftendom. Hence, whilft the *papal clergy* croaked like frogs (*unclean fpirits* through the contaminating influence of kingly prerogative embracing the maid, originally pure and heaven-

born) in the papal administration, it pleased GOD
that the national rod should put them to silence.
Before, therefore, many more speeches are made,
and sympathetic exclamations are sent abroad respecting their extermination, let it be proved that
the papal clergy did not, in the prophetic field,
stand exactly exposed to the stroke they received!
They were *unclean.* Their offerings were un-
savory. unclean flesh was in their garments.

THIS exposition of the prophetic figure can
not be confuted. It challenges all the powers of
papal or protestant Rome, of the mother of harlots and of all her daughters to wash themselves
clean from the contamination which this prophetic construction fastens upon them.

LET **our pen** be forgiven if it say, that the
tripple **exertion** of power in the dark shade of
things, in the regions of mystical Babylon, is
an off-set and counterpart to the tripple exertion of the Trinity, in unity, in the pure and
unadulterated offices of our holy religion.——
As the exertion of this power maintains and
preserves the true worshippers of GOD in the
paths of purity, truth, and holiness; so, as a
counterpart, in point operation, it pleases GOD
to let the **three** *unclean spirits go forth unto the
kings of the earth and of the whole world together*

D

*er them to the battle of that great day of GOD
ALMIGHTY.* This operation is now performing.

The exposition comes to confider,

2. THE courfe of this operation. They go
forth to the *kings of the earth and of the whole
world.*

THE love of dominion *in kings :* the partici-
pation of it in *priefly* eftablifhments, founds the
alarm at their prophetic mouth ; rings the tocfin thro' all their realms, and calls forth all under their influence *to the battle of the great* **day** *of*
GOD ALMIGHTY. That a combination between
the kings and priefts of the earth is formed, none
will deny. That ftate calls upon **the church,**
and that church calls upon the ftate, is feen in all
the regions of myftical Babylon. Come up, fay
they, one to the other, to the help of the LORD
againft the mighty, for CHURCH and STATE *are
in danger !*

This declaration will not be denied. The
deftruction of them both fo far as to diffolve this
union, is written in the great decree. The former verfe is a declaration to this point, whilft the
going forth of the unclean fpirits is the mode of
fummoning up the waters of Babylon to the
mark of perdition. *And the fixth angel poured
out his vial upon the great river Euphrates and the*

waters thereof was dried up, that the way of the kings of the east might be prepared. The river Euphrates by its waters, its trade, its wealth supported old Babylon. Its waters were dried up, and the Medes and Persians, the kings of the East took the city. The present Euphrates is the faith, the treasures, the power of mystical Babylon. **This river is** drying up. People have much less confidence in kingly and priestly **power,** in *iron and clay* establishments than they used to have. They have been, like old Israel in bondage long enough. They care not for the waters of old Babylon. Let the kings of the East come in! let the means which GOD hath appointed to shake down the walls of Babylon prosper! let all nations be shaken, that the *desire of all nations may come!*—**The** two leaved gates of mystical Babylon are the double exertion, the combined operations of kingly and priestly power. Let the door-posts be struck down, and let the captives come forth!

THE impossibility of any other constructions, establishes the foregoing to be the true and genuine meaning of the passage.

THE stile of *unclean* is of prophetic or figurative cast. It is taken from the ordinances of Jewish service. Certain animals, persons, and things, were stiled *unclean.* They were not accepted in, or purified for the service of GOD, according to the Jewish ritual. The ox was a *clean* beast, and might be offered in sacrifice; but the ass was *unclean*, and might not be brought into the courts of the LORD's House. In a prophetic sense these things prefigure the purity of the persons and service maintained in the Gospel Law. The offerings must be *pure*: otherwise they are *unclean*. The offerings of a priesthood, held forth by the arm of national or political power are *unclean*. Their persons and services are contaminated. They are unholy; they are impure. The intoxitating cup of mystical Babylon is the " cup of blessing" which they hold forth. It is a mixed cup. The wine presented is the wine of a kingly and of a priestly communion. This cup in a prophetic sense, is called the cup of *demons*, or of devils. It is an *unnatural, mixed* and *beastly* cup. Its wine is disgorged from the mouth of the *Dragon !* of the *beast*, and of the *false prophet.* It is not the simple, pure and holy cup which proceeds from the united administration of the FATHER, SON, and HOLY GHOST. It is a counterfeit, bastardly, and beastly cup. It is that cup which indignant Heaven is now striking from the hand of papal Rome. Kings and cardinals cannot keep their hand steady. The intoxicating bowl is broken and breaking. The " golden cup," in

the head of the myſtical woman, " full of abo-
minations and filthineſs of her fornicatoin" is to
be ſtruck to the ground. *For all nations have
drunk of the wine of the wrath of her fornication
and the kings of the earth have committed fornication with her, and the merchants of the earth are
waxed rich, th'o' the abundance of her delicacies.
And I heard another voice from heaven ſaying, come
out of her my people that ye be not partakers of
her ſins and that ye receive not of her plagues.*

THE cup of this connexion is called the cup of
demons or devils. Thus ſaith the apoſtle, in reſpect to the mixture of the goſpel ſervice with
the heatheniſh inſtitutions. *Ye cannot be partakers, of the cup of the LORD and of the cup of
devils.*—This combined cup goes forth to *the
kings of the earth and of the whole world to gather
them to the battle of that great day of GOD AL-
MIGHTY.*

IT gathers them by the ſtrength of its wine ;
by its fondneſs for, and anxiety to maintain its
former prerogative ; and, laſtly, it gathers them
to meet the deſtiny which they are appointed to
receive in that *great day of GOD ALMIGHTY.*
The day refered to, is the preſent day : ſo filled
from the magnitude of the events the ſcene diſ-
cloſes : from the ſeverity of the wrath of GOD

E

upon the seat of the beast, and from regard to
the stupendous scenes which are to follow in
quick succession. That the scriptures might be
fulfilled, and the shafts of the ALMIGHTY have
an object at which to aim their unerring indignation, it was necessary that suitable means
should be employed to rally up the forces of the
uncircumcised, to meet the rod of the GOD of
Jacob. The croakings of kingly power, at the
lips of a contaminated priesthood, have marve-
loufly fulfilled the scriptures, and presented the
huntsmen of the ALMIGHTY, their prey. A
conspiracy !— a conspiracy ! against all the estab-
lished governments and religions, in the world,
is on foot, they cry !—from what quarter, it is
demanded ?— from the unprincipled revolution-
tionists : from Talleyrand and his associates, they
answer ! a fact, not denied ! a fact indeed ! a
conspiracy exists ! Let the proofs of a Robinson
cut their way !—But who hath suffered the foundation of this conspiracy to be so *deeply laid* ?
to be so *artfully* managed ? to be so *successfully*
played off ?—undoubtedly, it is done under the
superintendance of that prophetic eye, which
saw that the time was come to make good the
predictions of holy writ. The vassals of the
dragon, of the beast, and of the false prophet
must be summoned up to open war ; whilst the
secret underminings of Robinson's conspirators

weaken the roots of those apostate cedars which the stormy wind, *fulfilling his will* is appointed to bear away !—In this view it is easy to see why the cedars of the apostate Jerusalem are so easily shaken : why the calves of Dan and Bethel are so easily thrown down. The croakings around these calves, are like the cuttings of the prophets of Baal, agonizing that their god would come and confound the instruments who bear so awful and so successful a commission against their craft. never were the pulpits of Rome papal, and of Rome protestant so warmly plied with antidote against the threatened indignation as at the present time. The theme is worn out : the subject is grown stale : and if the combination between kingly and priestly power is to come down, the people begin to say *let it fall ! let it fall !* No fear for the truth of GOD ; seeing the *iron band* with the *green grass* is already applied to the Assyrian stump !—

THE exposition of the figurative language respecting the *three unclean spirits* may be supported, in its application to the ministration of mystical Babylon by appeal to Doct. Dwight's discourse on the fourth of July 1798. see p. 6. "in the remaining verses &c"

THE exposition of the doctor is good ; and he needs only to make the same application of the croakings of the frogs to the " regular clergy" of the proteftant hierarchy that he does to the papal clergy, and he will difcover his own ftanding to be not far removed from the order of the ecclefiaftical frogs againft whom his expofition is fo juftly fevere.

To avoid the application, it is eafy to fee that the doctor attempts to put the cap of this illuftration, eventually upon thofe who now appear as the fappers and miners of the old hierarchy. Thefe he fays are the followers of Voltaire, of the mafonic order, and of the Illuminati. But by what kind of logic the doctor will prove that an application of prophetic character, defignating the combination of the DRAGON, of the BEAST and of the *falfe prophets*, as conftituting the ecclefiaftical hierarchy, can be laid at the door of thofe infidels appointed of GOD to ftrike down that hierarchy, it is not eafy to determine! the doctor muft look over the College library once more. There is a wide difference between the hierarchy of tumbling Rome, and the inftruments confpiring and warring againft it.

WHETHER it is not probable that the hierarchy of Rome was capable of producing the prophetic frogs in queftion may be in fome meafure determined by an appeal to their character in a thankfgiving difcourfe of Rev. N. Strong, 1798.

" After having made these observations, to
secure myself against the imputation of a rigorous
and uncharitable spirit, I must be allowed freely
to say, that the Roman empire in all its forms,
the ancient and modern, the civil and ecclesiastical, hath been a tyrannical and persecuting
power. It is unquestionably the same power
pointed out in the gospel prophecies, by the man
of sin—by the beast—the mother of harlots—the
false prophet—the beast that ascended out of the
bottomless pit and endeavored to destroy the
witnesses of God—the dragon that cast out of
his mouth a flood of water to destroy the truth
of God—the modern Babylon which should fall
by the signal judgments of God—that great
city that ruleth over the kings of the earth."

And again, p. 21. " Its tyranny hath been
over its own subjects and the people of distant
regions. To a civil despotism, which naturally
grew out of the barbarous foundation of feudal
rights, it hath added a religious tyranny beyond
all the sins that have before defiled the earth or
oppressed men. It hath blasphemicusly changed
and used the religion of the meek and lowly Jesus to scourge oppressed nations—to dethrone
lawful princes—and to indulge and pardon the
worst of subjects in the greatest crimes. The
civil and religious tyrant, have walked hand in

hand to deceive, to impoverish, & to enslave the
soul & then to hail the whole as done for the glory
of God. These prophecies of John had a vast
object for their description. Not merely one city, or nation or century of time; but the great
political body of Europe, with its dependencies
in other quarters of the globe, which is the old
Roman empire arisen in a new form, consisting
of popes, ecclesiastical states and dignities, pro-
fessed apostles of Jesus at the head of armies, em-
perors, kings, princes, and a multifarious cata-
logue of civil and ecclesiastical courts, dignities,
powers and oppressions. This vast body has been
called the holy Roman church, and the holy Roman empire with its allies."

And yet Mr. Strong readily coincides with
" Timothy Dwight," in saying that he hath
fully explained the three impure spirits under
the first vial that went out of the *mouth* of the
dragon, and out of the *mouth* of the beast, and
out of the mouth of the false prophet to mean
the principles of infidelity " which within a century have arisen in the old christian world."—If
the *mouth* of the dragon *kingly* power—the *mouth*
of the beast *priestly* power combined, and of the
mouth of the false prophet, the impure testimony
of this combination disgorge only principles of
infidelity, will Mr. Strong have any objections

that this communion be *forsaken* throughout the world, tho' it preach under a protestant name!

To parry this conclusion perhaps Mr. S. may appeal to a sentence in his discourse p. 17 —" It is the Talleyrands in character, and their associates, whom I conceive to be most properly designated by the *mother of harlots*, in the present period of the great apostacy from GOD." This appropriation of the " mother of harlots" to Talleyrand and his associates was, *politically needful*, in order to justify the idea that the impure testimony of the dragon, beast and false prophet might be said to proceed out of their mouth.— But alas! for this subterfuge! Old commentators who have never had their heads turned by the vertigo of modern whirlwinds, will testify that the " mother of harlots" had been on the stage twelve hundred years before Talleyrand was born! neither can all the artifice of Mr. Strong invent how the administration of Talleyrand forms the least shade of resemblance to the apostate empire of the *dragon*, the *beast* and *false prophet*; or, in his own words, to the " mother of harlots." They are no more alike than the game pursued, is like the hounds that croud the chase. The mystical mother, who with her daughters of every communion, sitteth upon the many waters committing fornication with " the kings of the earth" is the prey : Talleyrand and his associates are the rapacious pack to whom it is given to take the prey, and to divide the spoil.— Church and state policy form the *antichristian fish* which this Leviathan pursues.

Mr. Strong, must therefore throw his die once more, or it will be pronounced that, **as yet**, it falls from a trembling hand.

But, perhaps, these two prelates may get aid, from the puffy sanction of their brother Doct. Morse. This Doctor in divinity, whether to save his falling brother, or, by puffing his superiors, to mount with them the Theological car, and ride to the tune of the *Triumviri*, I will not decide, has lavished forth his most hearty Amen to the spirit of the two discourses just now quoted.— How far the two gentlemen will acknowledge the debt of gratitude to their trumpeter I will not undertake to determine. If it should be found that a Triumvirate was, absolutely, formed in New England, and that the prophetic figure, literally, hath its application already manifest, perhaps it would be difficult to prove that the figure did **not** apply to the three persons forming the Triumvirate in question : who, it may be said, is more fond, or doth more for the support of *kingly* prerogative, than Timothy Dwight ! who assumes more theological & political airs, than the presiding bishop of the day, N. Strong ? & who can dance to all tunes, & preach to all texts relating to church and state policy, with a readier hand than Jedediah Morse !—Is not the prophetic character fairly illustrated !—out of the mouth of the *dragon* ; out of the mouth of the *beast* and out of the mouth of the *false prophet.* These characters form the trinity of church and state policy. Let us see how well the chief speaker, the third and last great acting character can play his part !—

THAT the attempt to place the shades of this dark character to the *regular clergy* of the polit-ical establishments, in protestant countries may not be pronounced unfair let it be premised that these gentlemen make no apology for the appro-priation of the croaking character to the *regu-lar clergy* of the *papal* church. The only quest-ion, to be settled, is whether a priestly admini-stration, in the arms of protestant kings, is not as justly entitled to the charge of mystical for-nication, to the character of *political creakers,* as the papal clergy themselves : especially as Mr. Strong gives great credit to the papal clergy for the constancy of their faith. " three unclean spirits, like frogs" says doctor Dwight, are ex-hibited as coming out of the mouth of the drag-

E

on or devil; of the beaſt, or Romiſh government, and of the falſe prophet; or as I appre-
hend, of the *regular clergy of that hierarchy!*"

LET us now attend to the political ſong of
the chief croaker in favor of a *ſafe eccleſiaſtical
lodgment* in the arms of " the kings of the earth"
juſt now hinted at.

IN a faſt-ſermon; the ſaid Morſe, in view
of the effects of that reformation in church concerns, which it ſeems, evidently, the will of heaven to accompliſh, cries out *if the foundations be
deſtroyed what can the righteous do?* Indeed, it
may be anſwered, *what ſhall they do?* But who
are theſe righteous perſons?—In the ſpirit of
this national diſcourſe—they are the righteous
clergy of all countries, where the revolutionary
ſtorm ſweeps away their **political places**—their *ſal-
aries—taxes,* and all kingly ſupport! indeed
if ſuch foundations be deſtroyed *what ſhall the
righteous do?* " In ſome of our newſpapers"
ſaith Morſe, " which are read with more avidity, and more faith than the Holy Bible, they
(the clergy) are continually *reproached and vili-
fied;* and every low artifice is uſed to leſſen
their influence and uſefulneſs; and what is deeply to be lamented, this poiſon is greedily ſwal-
lowed, and aſſiduouſly diſſeminated by ſome,

even who profefs to be *the warm friends and supporter of chriftianity, and of the chriftian miniftry."* If this pathetic exclamation be juft, it can fcarcely be doubted that the good people of all communions, begin to diftinguifh between *real gofpel minifters,* and political croakers.—But if things go on fo, what fhall thefe *righteous men* do? The anfwer is ready: Let fome of them *write poetry,* others, *follow their diftilleries;* and the reft *write geographies.*—But if rather than do this, they infift on croaking; let them take a moving pofition, and as Talleyrand advances (of whom they feem to be in fuch fear) and like one of Morfe's alligators opens his mouth for prey, let them *dragon, beaft and falfe prefth* t altogether, make one defperate leap into the yawning Hell of this gaping Leviathan: I will anfwer for it, that the upper jaw fhall fall with all the avidity of the alligator fecuring his prey!—a fweet morfel thefe croakers would prove, in the voracious maw of the infatiable Talleyrand.

THAT this is the game, fuccefsfully purfued, by the accufers of the day, is acknowledged by Morfe: "The clergy have been among the firft victims to that fanguinary revolutionising fpirit which now convulfes the world." And can this croaker give a better reafon for the

succefs of th's revolutioni ing fplrit, than that
there is a j in. on formed both of *external* and
of *hidlen* operation according to the will of GOD
whereby the whore is to be hated, to be made
defolate and naked—her flefh to *be eaten* and her
b ody *burnt with fire*—for *ftrong is the LORD GOD
who judgeth her*.

WHETHER, therefore, a *moving pofition* does
not become the croaker in queftion let fober
fenfe determine.

BUT againft the judicious and well-informed
of his own ftate, this chief fpeaker takes up his
burthen, and exclaims, " fo numerous, indeed,
and bold have the adverfaries of the clergy become, fo confident of their ftrength, that even
in *our legiflature*, they have lately *ventured* to
bring forward, and ftrenuoufly to advocate mea-
fures, and publickly to *avow opinions*, tending directly, and almoft, *infallibly*, to deprive a great
part of the prefent clergy of *regular fupport!!*"

How aftonifhing that, in the legiflature of
Maffachufetts there fhould be found men who
fhould *venture* to avow, and *ftrenuoufly advocate*
mealures tending *almoft infallibly*, to deprive
thefe *regular croakers, of regular fupport* ! !—O
tempora ! O mores !

THE anfwer to this, *piteous*, *felffh*, and *fearful*

exclamation is found in the well acknowledged
sentiment, that the pure gospel of the ever blessed
Redeemer, does not depend on the *legal stipends*
of an *hired priesthood* for its support : and though
Jedediah Morse might not be of that opinion,
it seems the legislature of Massachusetts were
well nigh ready to put the question to the test.

But how astonished will the candid of all denominations of christians be when they come to
be informed that the *sum total* of the bill before
the legislature was calculated only to give that
liberty of conscience to distinct worshippers of
God, which our Federal Constitution secures,
and which finds no enemies, excepting in those
who still abide by the exploded doctrine of the
unity and infallibility of mystical Rome !

The whole of this *mighty nothing* is found in
Morse's own words, in a note at the end of his
discourse, " Note D. " The measures alluded
to in the foregoing paragraph were proposed to
the legislature during the last session in the form
of a bill, which was supported with much zeal
by some of the members. The purport of this
bill, as I have been informed, from very respect-
able authority, was that any individual producing a certificate from the clerk of any association
of men for religious purposes, that he or she, act-

G

ually contributed to the support of public worship, should exempt such person from all legal
assessments or requisitions, for the maintenance
of public teachers.

"HAD this bill passed into a law, it is easy to see
that it would have justified and protected (as
was no doubt the intention of **the bill, tho' by**
no means of all who may have voted **for** it) the
disaffected, the irreligious and the despisers of
public worship and **of** the christian sabbath, in
every town and parish, in withdrawing that support of the christian ministry which the laws
now oblige them to give. **This** class of people is not small in many of our towns and parish-
es; and their support taken away would **reduce**
many **of** the clergy **to a** situation that would
compel them to leave their people."

THE charge of design in the framers of the
bill to justify the *disaffected*, and *irreligious* and
the *despisers* of publick worship &c.—looks a lit-
tle harsh, when it is known, that many who are
not tied up to the trap-stick work of state establishments are, perhaps, as conscientious worship-
ers of GOD as any who are compelled to worship,
thro' the force of a constable's execution. But
the heavy charge is; they were to be justified
in *withdrawing that support of the christian ministry which the laws now oblige them to give !—2.*

las! how will pure and undefiled religion be endangered when thefe political croakers fhall be deprived of their ftipends!—will infidelity itfelf pretend that the dew of Heaven is all exhaufted?—or that the clouds can give no more rain? Let the jaw of Talleyrand receive thefe frogs; that opportunity may be afforded for the pure and undefiled fervice of God! to make itfelf manifeft!—fuch a law the ftate of Connecticut paffed eight years ago; and now, a tul to tell, the ftate of Maffachufetts are about to follow the fame example! on this account this political croaker founds the alarm: cries out of the progrefs of mafonry; of the illuminati, and of confpiracy againft priefts!—one would think him poffeffed of *full information*; that the ftate of Connecticut was *already* fwallowed up and that the tocfin was already founding; that the flight of wifdom, from the counfels of Maffachufetts, was at hand!—alas for fuch croakers! nothing can be plead in their behalf but *the trepidation* in which they confefs themfelves to be. Hear the confeffion of this man! " I am aware" fays he " that for thofe gloomy forebodings and for this vindication of the clergy, I may by fome, be called *vifionary, fplenetic, credulous, and felfifh*"—Let any reader of his book fay, if ever man clothed himfelf with a more becoming gar-

ment ! at leaſt, by the conſtant ſkippings and
croakings of this *credulous viſionary*, it might well
be judged that he heard the howlings of Talleyrand's pack at the front door, and ſaw the
huntſmen ready to receive him in the rear !

BUT leſt, before the honeſt ſtrictures of our
pen had gone thro' with an examination of the
viſionary ſchemes, and ematiated defence of this
political croaker ; he ſhould get ſuch a pelting as
to fall from his poſt, and perhaps obtain friends,
thro' compaſſion ; the NATIONAL FAST *ſermon* is
diſcharged ; information being given ; that the
mean apologies—the unmeaning bows and crin-
ging ſupplications for pardon—the alarm about
ſecret ſocieties which do not exiſt—the unquali-
fied reproaches of the maſonic order, who never
dreamed of their political conſequence, much-
leſs of any *political defection* from the general in-
intereſt until taught that they were capable of
it by this performance ; ſhall be again taken up
and *daſhed in the face* of this croaker, the next
time the ſwelling of his bladder gives notice that
his head is above water.

STONE againſt the IMAGE No. XXIV.

A CONFESSION,

At the bar of the ecclesiastical counsels of the State of Connecticut.

SIRS,

Understanding that it hath been moved in one of your bodies, that, *on confession*, the undersigned might be received to the fellowship of your councils and communion; I have thought proper to pen the following; which is submitted for your consideration.

CONFESSION is made, that until Feb. 5th, 1796, I walked in the service and fellowship of your communion, so far as my licenture for public service by you; and so far as my ordination, by the presbytery of New York, in your connection, gave me a standing with you. Foreseeing with you, that the signs of the times predicted something favorable to the house of GOD, I was led to use my influence in uniting the brethren of different denominations, as much as possible, into one body, that the general and universal fellowship, expected, might be promoted. whilst occupied in collecting discourses for publication, in maintaining extensive correspondencies on the subject of promoting the general interest of religion, following up the same by maintaining a circuit of preaching for forty miles, in the vicinity of Elifabethtown ; it pleafed GOD to give me to underſtand that no millennial profpects were to be realifed under the mixed, mutilated, and apoſtate condition in which the external or- der of the vifible houſehold, then was. A fe- ceffion from the connexion in which I ſtood was' infiſted on ; that I might return to the doctrine, precept and example of the great Redeemer in the pattern ſhewed in the mount.—I proclaimed myſelf " independant of the Preſbytery, of the Syſ od, and of the general Affembly."—I faid that the preſbyterian order, as a body, had its origin in the pattern of the Scottiſh church : that this church, by the ſardings and daubings of acts of parliament, with which the old confeffion of faith was full, proved itſelf to belong to the an- tichriſtian family ; many in Scotland pronouncing the Kirk of Scotland in its texure, & appendages to form a very prominent feature in the field of prophetic apoſtacy. The reception of the kings commiffion fitting with his drawn fword at the right hand of the moderator of the Gene- ral Affembly—the right of ariſtocrat prefentation and the power to enforce fuch prefentation to livings in the face of the choice and wiſhes of the people, at the point of the bayonet, ſufficient- ly proves the connexion with kingly power, and evinces the ſpiritual tyranny which this church maintains :—as a fprout from this ſtump, the congregation over which I prefided poffeffed a charter given under royal hand and feal ; in which the officers of the church and the priveledges of the congregation were fpecified. being willing to acknowledge none as head of the church, in any form of ecclefiaftical adminiftration, but the LORD JESUS CHRIST, the Great Head of the church, I pronounced independence, and began to inftruct, and to organize upon the plan I judged truly fcriptural.

THE open declaration of independence of the prefbyterian connexion, brought a queftion before the congregation, whether, under fuch circumftances the connexion could be continued. The matter was refered to the prefbytery, foon to fit, at New York. Being warned of GOD of my duty to leave the place, I prepared myfelf for a removal and at the meeting of the prefbytery at New-York, was no my way to New England. Before the prefbytery I pronounced my willingnefs that they fhould take fuch notice of the reference from Elfabethtown as they thought proper : and , at the fame time, expreff d my determination to withdraw from the connexion and government of the prefbyterian church, a priveledge, which, as a prefbyterian, I had right to exercife.

In Connecticut, my public labors have, at times breathed the same spirit of independence; and have looked, in the illustration of the prophcies, at the independent state of the church which is at the door. My opinion is still firm and unshaken, that the day of GOD's great power is at hand; that his church will be purified, and washed from all the filthiness she hath contracted in her apostate condition; and that as soon as the church shall have made herself ready, the Great Bridegroom of the Heavens will appear for the espousal of his Bride. Furthering this object, and fulfilling the will of GOD, I think it incumbent to declare, that neither you nor your hearers can continue a moment longer in the state in which you are, without becoming exposed to the weighty sentence GOD hath pronounced against those who are found in connection with the administration of the *dragon*, of the *beast*, and of the *false prophet*. The passage of scripture calculated to throw light on this testimony, and to enforce it by penalties, awful as the pains of Hell, is found in Rev. XIV. 8, 12.

" 8 And there followed another angel, saying, Babylon is fallen, is fallen, that great city, because she made all nations drink of the wine of the wrath of her fornication.

9 And the third angel followed them, saying

with a loud voice, If any man worship the beast and his image, and receive his mark in his forehead, or in his hand,

10 The same shall drink of the wine of the wrath of GOD, which is poured out without mixture into the cup of his indignation; and he shall be tormented with fire and brimstone in the presence of the holy angels, and in the presence of the Lamb.

11 And the smoke of their torment ascendeth up for ever and ever: and they have no rest day nor night, who worship the beast and his image, and whosoever receiveth the mark of his name.

12 Here is the patience of the saints: here are they that keep the commandments of GOD, and the faith of JESUS.

THIS passage is designed to open the door of *separation* from the several communions and fellowships of worldly establishment, and to form, of all such as shall come out of their Babylonish estate, one *new, uniform* and *perfect church.* — The awful decree, just now cited, is designed to weaken the throne of the *beast* and of his *image*, and of all their instruments. The *worship* of the beast and of his image expresses the con-

dition of those who *yeild obeisance* to the empire
of the beast and of his Image ; or received *his
mark* in the *forehead* or in *the hand* : thus slaves
of old, were branded in their *forehead* and in
their hand to express to whom they appertained :
so, in these days, the mark received in the hand,
or in the forehead is the receiving the cup of
communion from the hand of any in the connexion of the kings of the earth ; or *being bap-
tized* ;receiving the *mark upon the forehead*, de-
noting that we are slaves to Babylon and devo-
ted to her service.——Hence, this is the moment
to make use of the interesting and affectionate
call : *come out of her my people that ye be not partakers in her sins, and that ye receive not of her
plagues !*

In the name of GOD the truth now advances,
that it may strike down all the fabricks of hu-
man and ecclesiastical invention, which have for
their foundation, or support any mixture of hu-
man inventions, not acknowledged in GOD's holy word. All are such whose standing would be
shook by the withdrawing of the hand of earth-
ly power, or support. If CHRIST's kingdom
hath not wisdom in its texture, oil in its horn,
and power from above, equal to a standing on
CHRIST the only foundation, let it fall to the
ground ! If the *prophetic, priestly* and *kingly* offi-

ces of the Redeemer are not sufficient for the defence of his honor, and the comfort of his people here below, it is not to be supposed that kingly power will aid to advance a cause, in its nature and design repugnant to their own wishes, otherwise than as it tends to the agrandizement of men in the forgetting of GOD.

THESE things, firs! I openly confess, and cheerfully avow, and am so far assured that these sentiments are gaining ground, every day that I am perfectly confident of their eventual success : especially whilst I know that the GOD of Heaven is now plying the engine of truth and of power, that men may know and obey, with growing alacrity, all his blessed will.

IN respect to the mode of induction into the new order of things it will be manifest to those who with becoming temper, may apply. A standard will be shortly raised ; to which, in a spiritual fence, the gathering of the people shall be.

In regard to civil power I believe it to be good in its place : in regard to things of this world. That the United States may see the salvation of GOD, thro' the touchings of his great power, is my expectation and hope : and dare to say there is a period, and an event not far distant in which the wisdom of GOD will be needful, and will not be witheld, in our outward concerns. Of this period, and of this event and of the happy effects, the Prefident of the United States will have full evidence in proper time! The God of Heaven will let the Prefident know that he hath other counfels of wifdom and of grace for this country, more than what can be obtained from the votaries of the beaft or of the falfe prophet.

DAVID AUSTIN, Junr.

☞ SHORTLY may be expected from the prefs, a *Mafonic* difcourfe ; entitled MASONRY, in its GLORY ; or the TEMPLE of SOLOMON, ILLUMINATED : in which attempt, it appears that the Temple of CREATION ; the GOSPEL TEMPLE, and the TEMPLE of SOLOMON are but one and the fame thing ; that they are but different modifications of the fame general adminiftration : that this fact needs only to be known ; to lead the votaries of natural religion, to fhake hands with the Chriftian and the Mafon. This done, a three fold cord will prefent itfelf, in behalf of the teftimony of God, not eafily to be broken. For this light, the children of men are waiting ; that the walls of feparation may be thrown down, and a fpirit of general fraternity, of peace on earth and of good will to men encompafs the globe !

THE whole is done in the light of feven lamps, fuftained by the golden candleftick of Zechariah, a figure of the feven fpirits which burn before the throne of GOD and of the LAMB.

www.ingramcontent.com/pod-product-compliance
Lightning Source LLC
Chambersburg PA
CBHW031823090426
42739CB00008B/1384